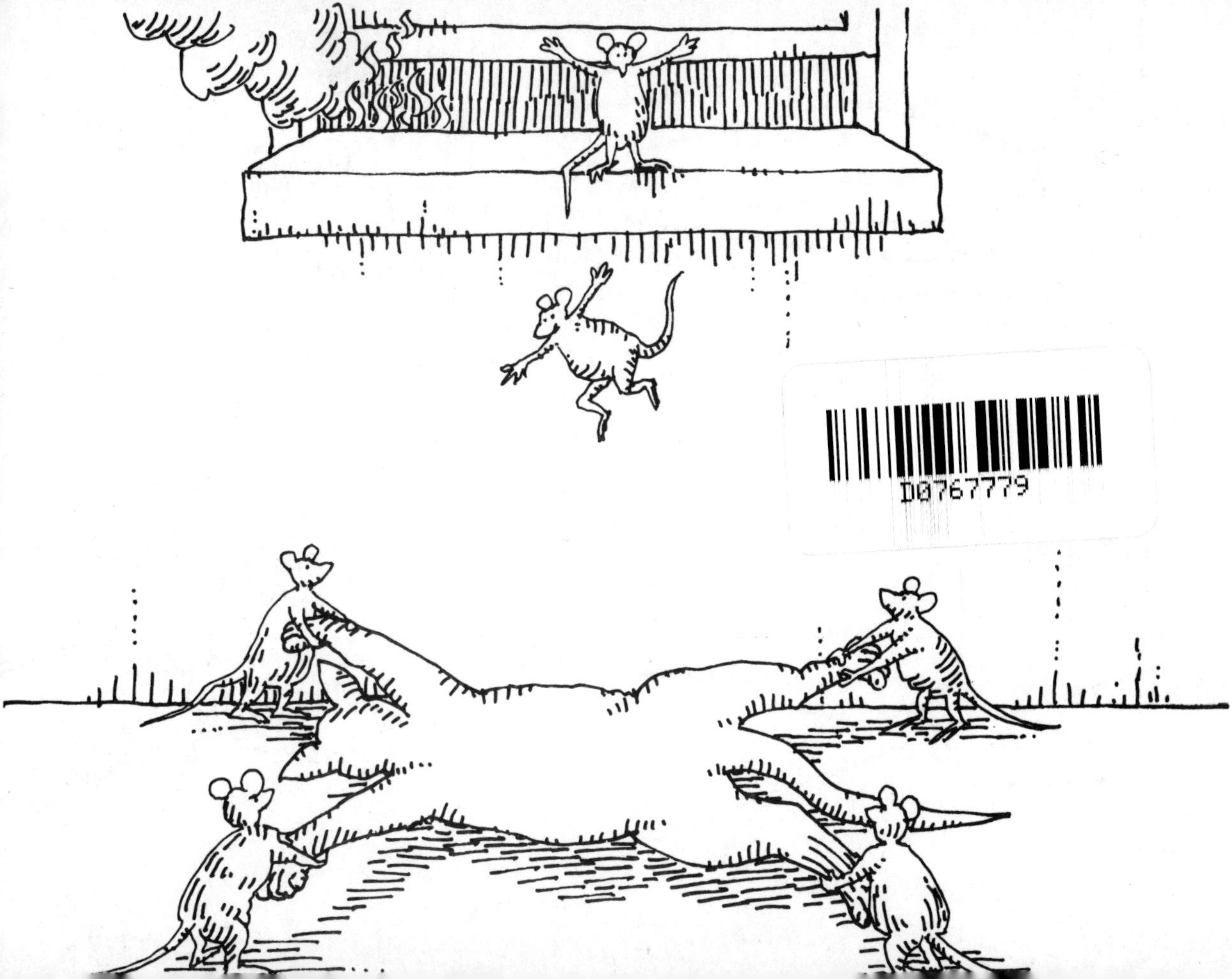

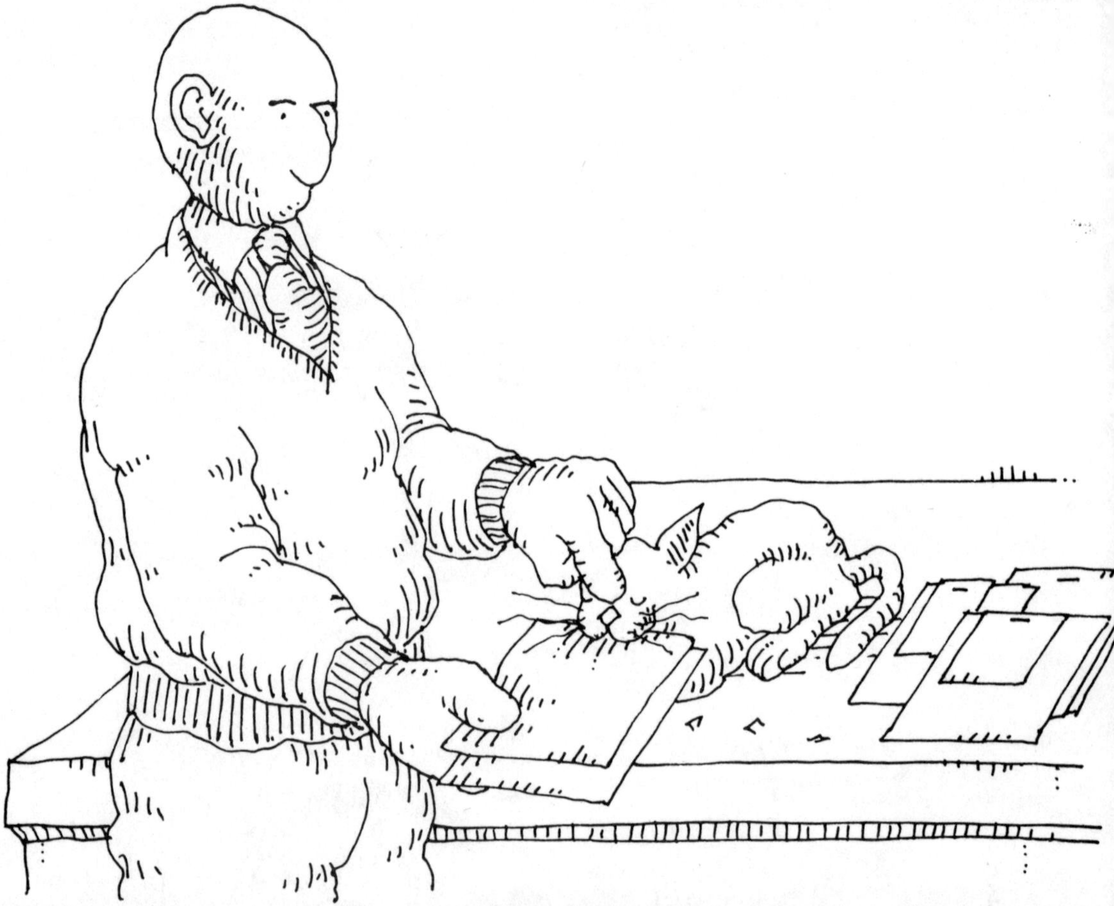

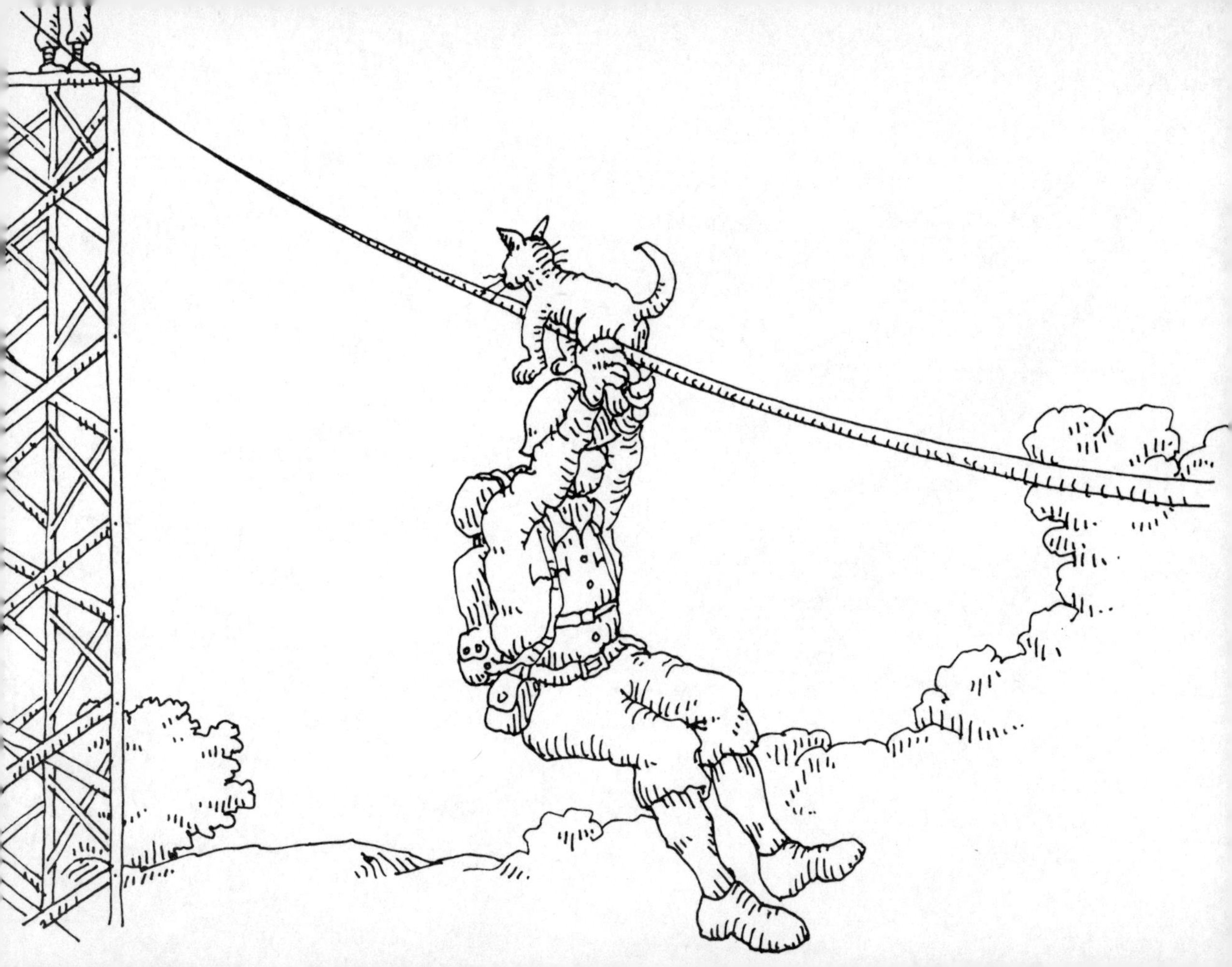

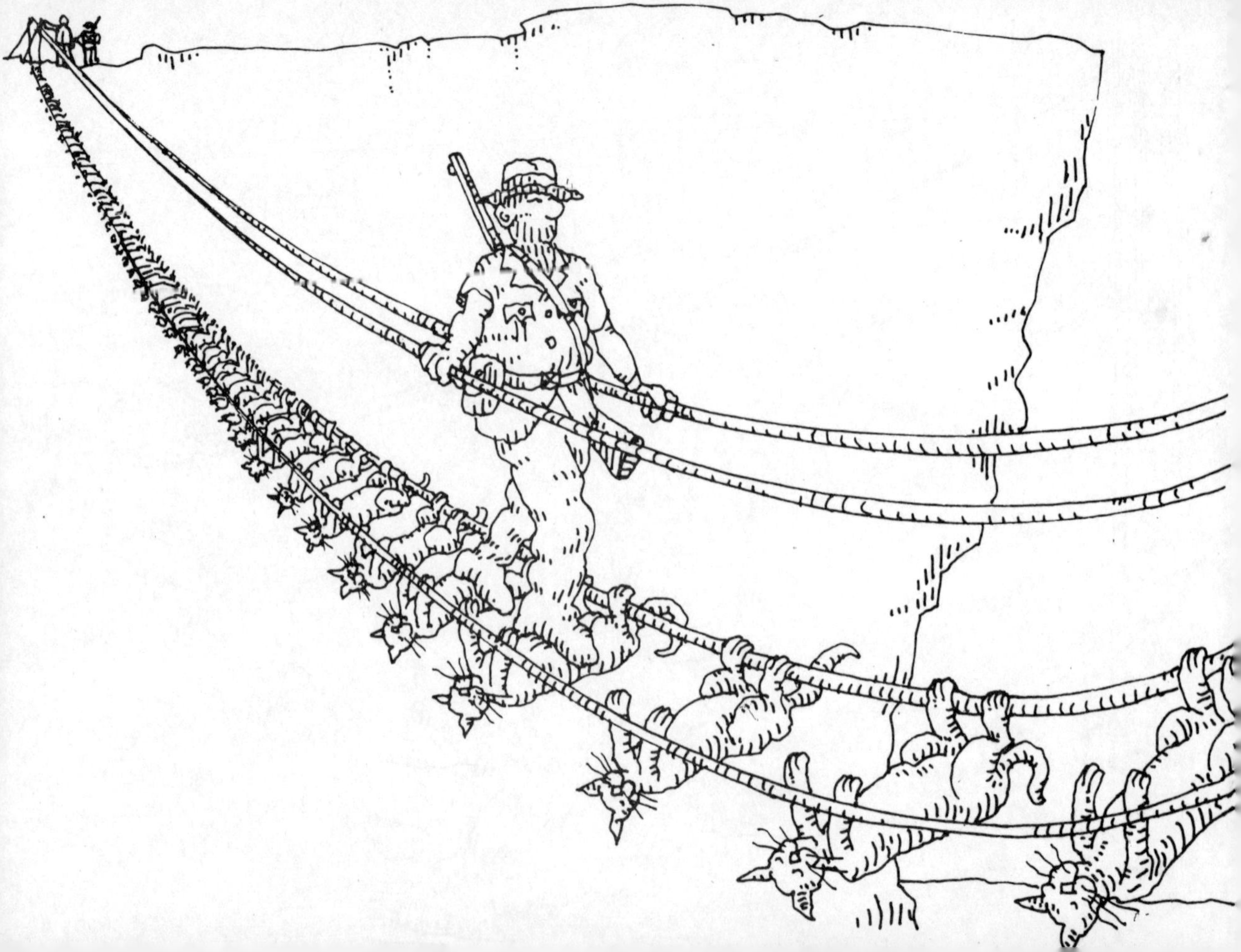

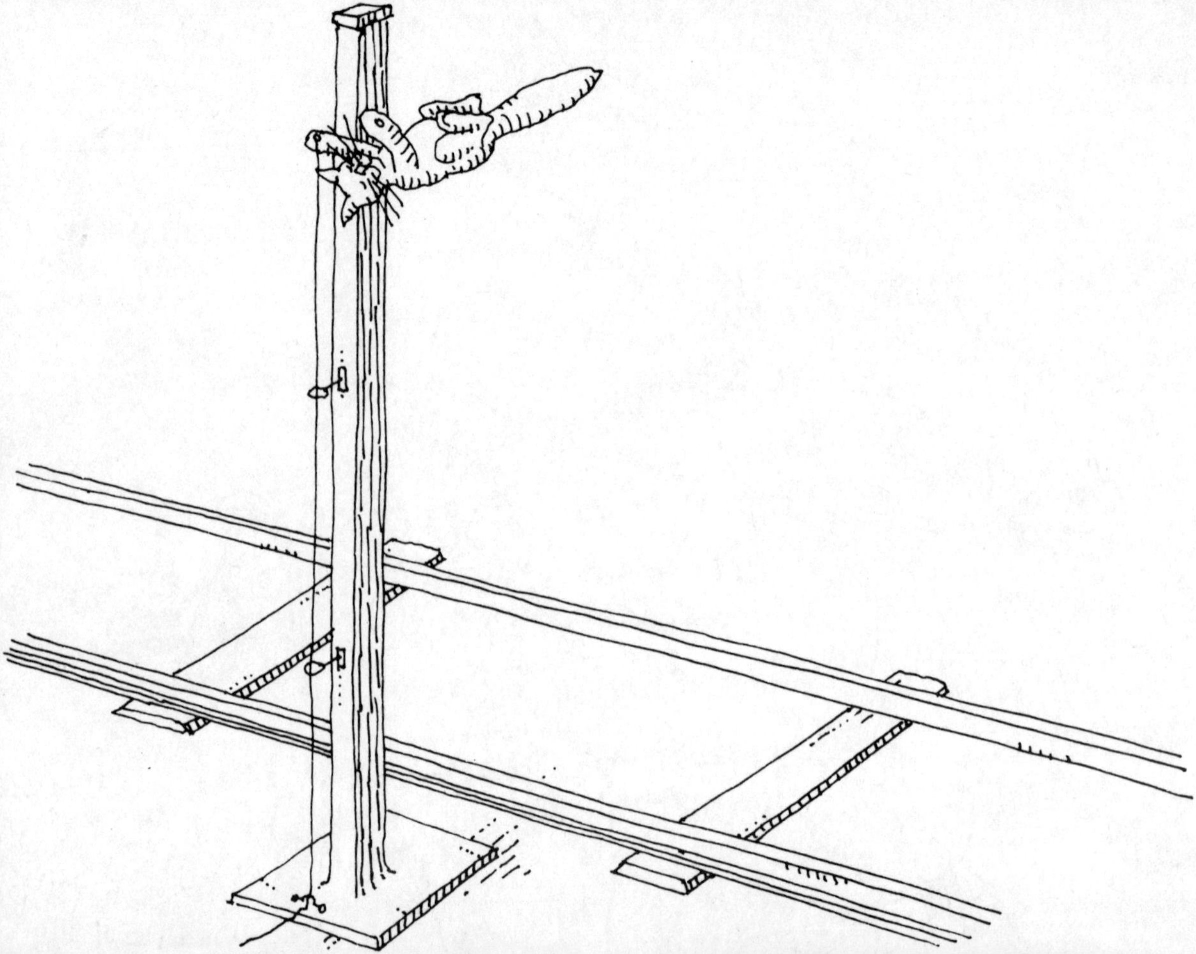

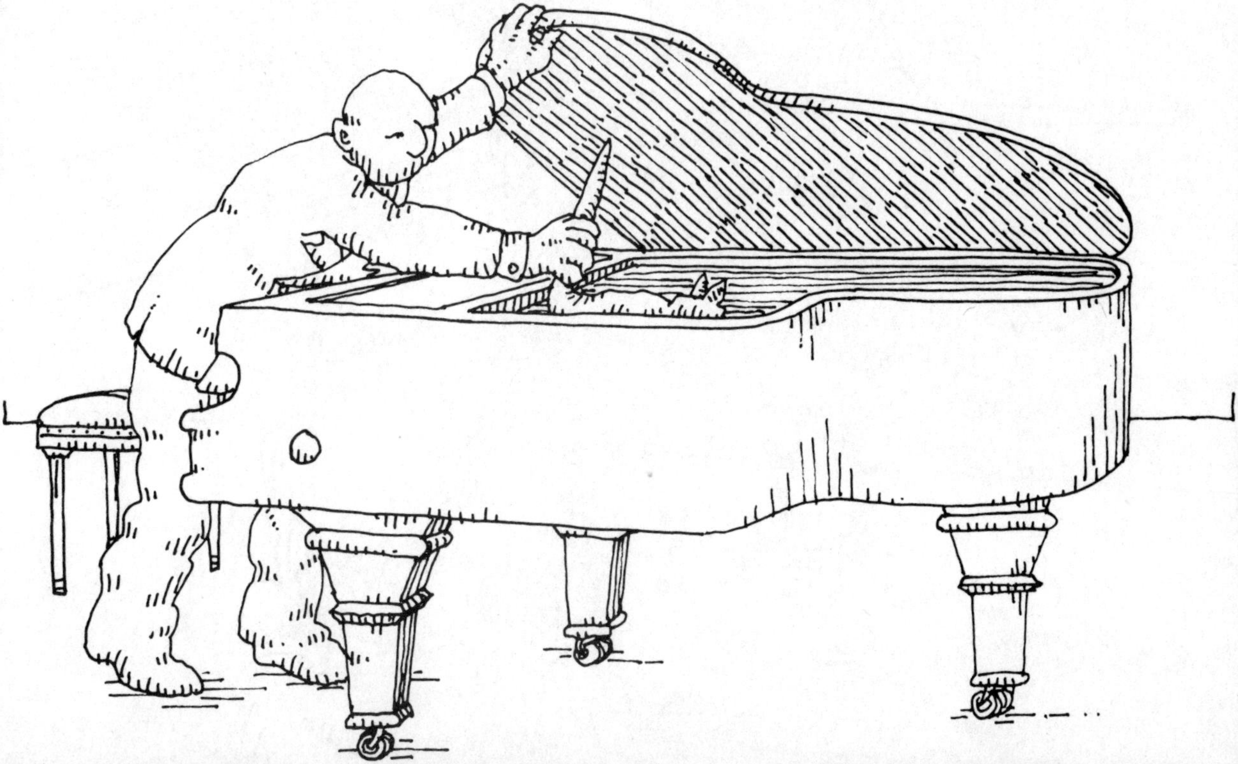

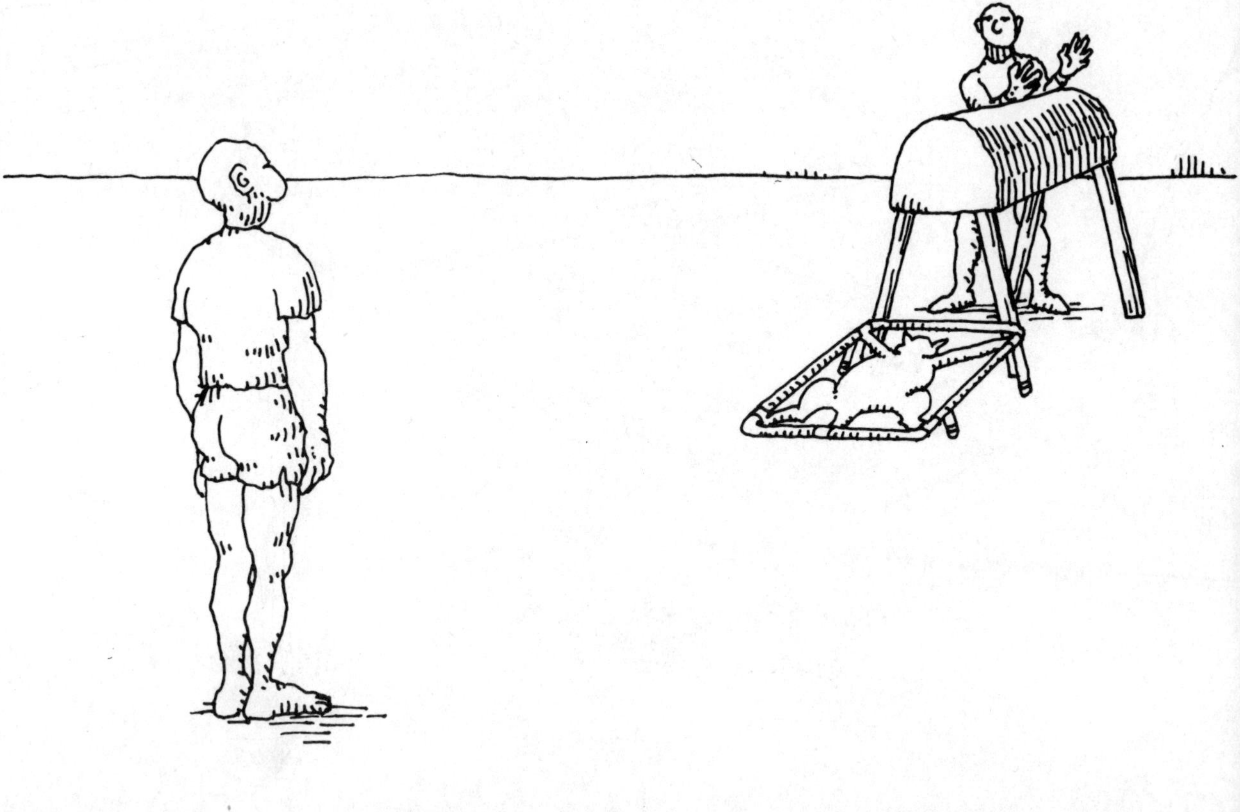

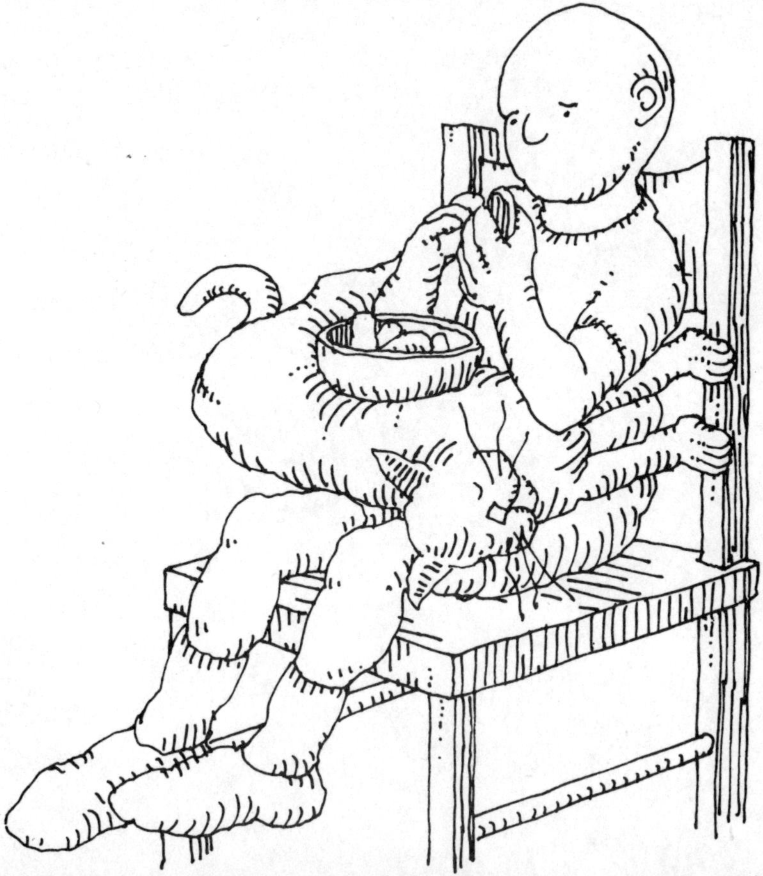

NFFC

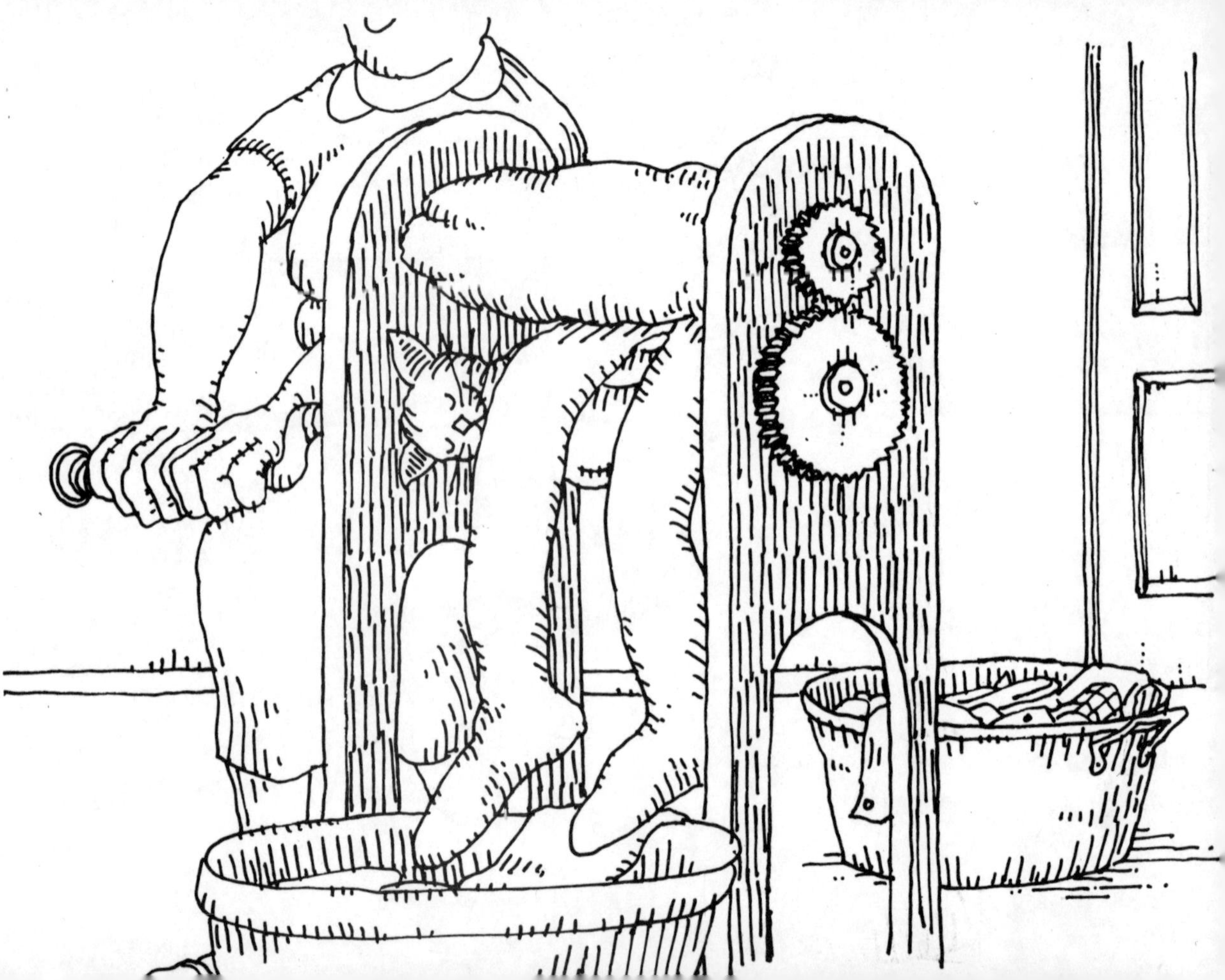

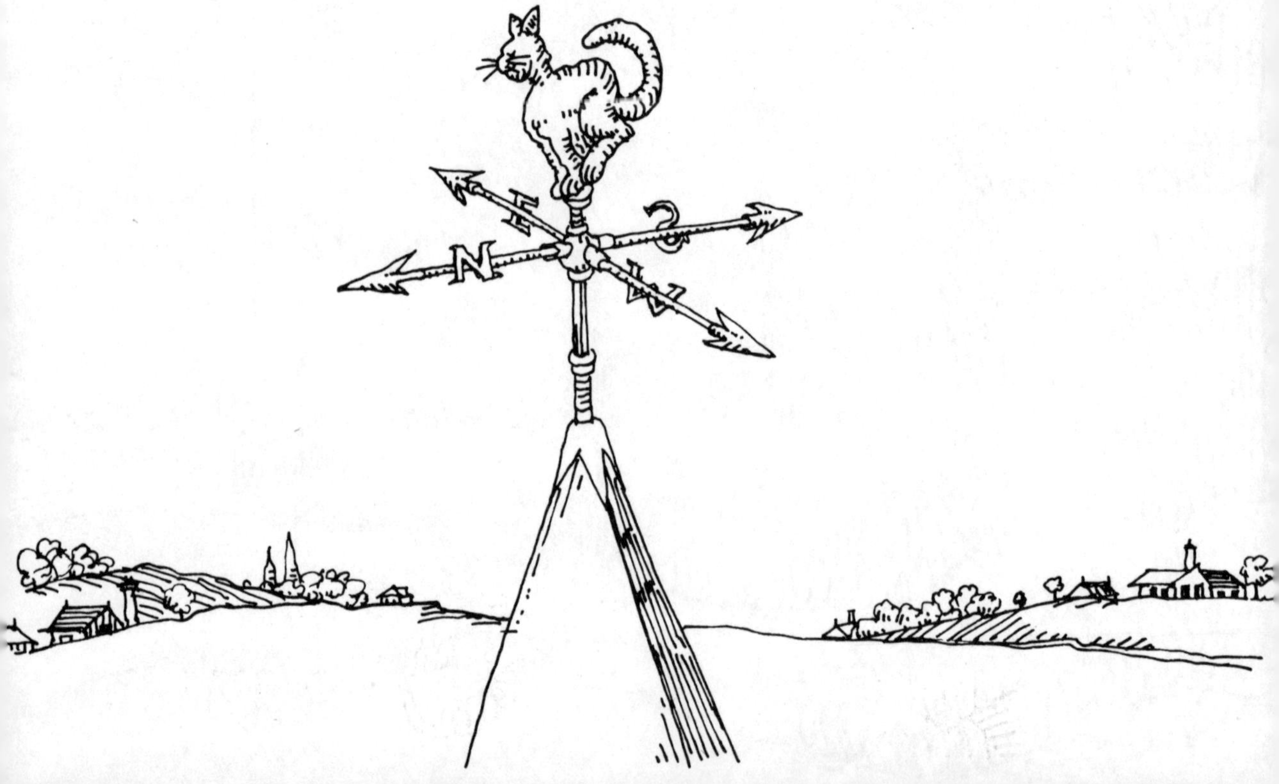
N
E
S
W

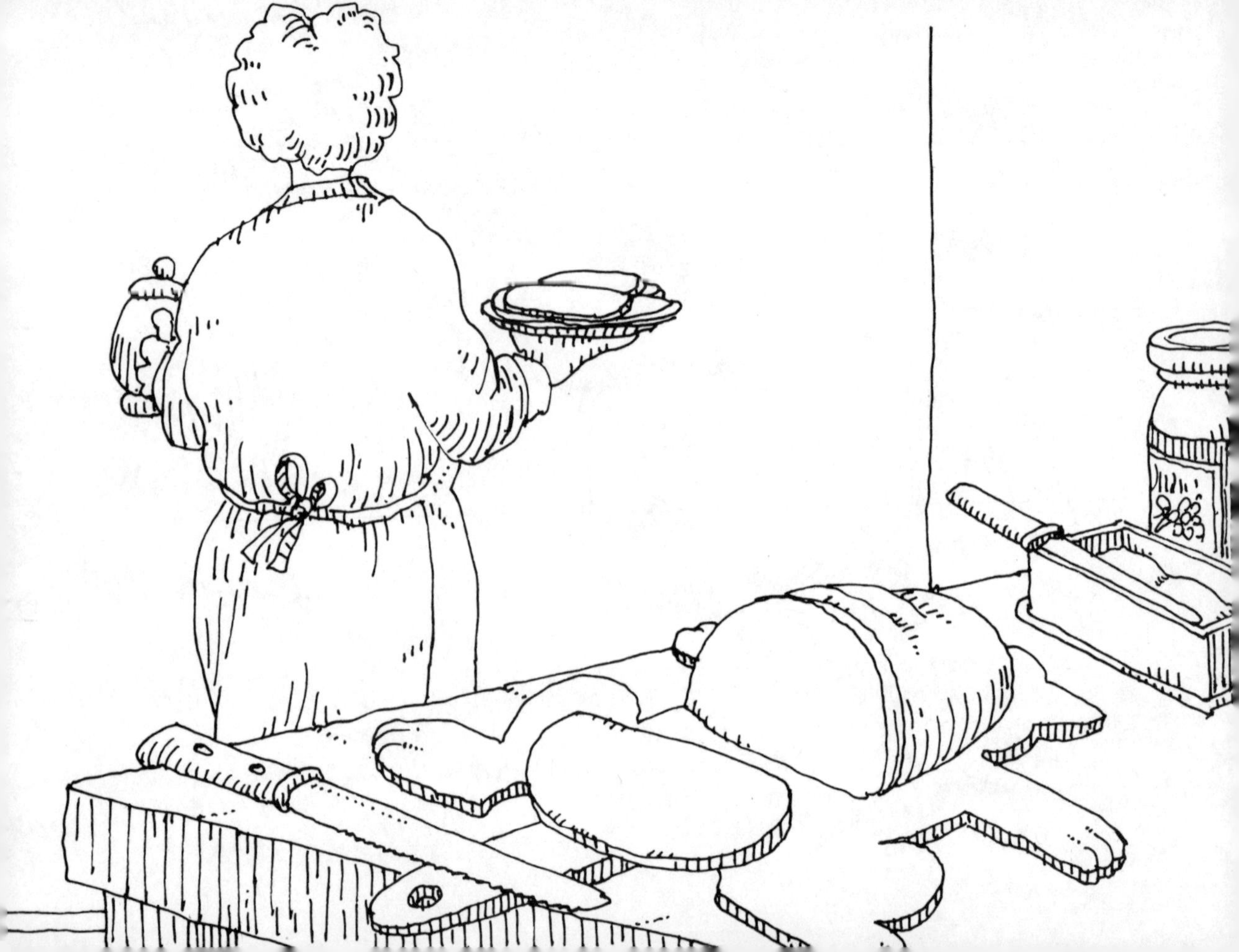

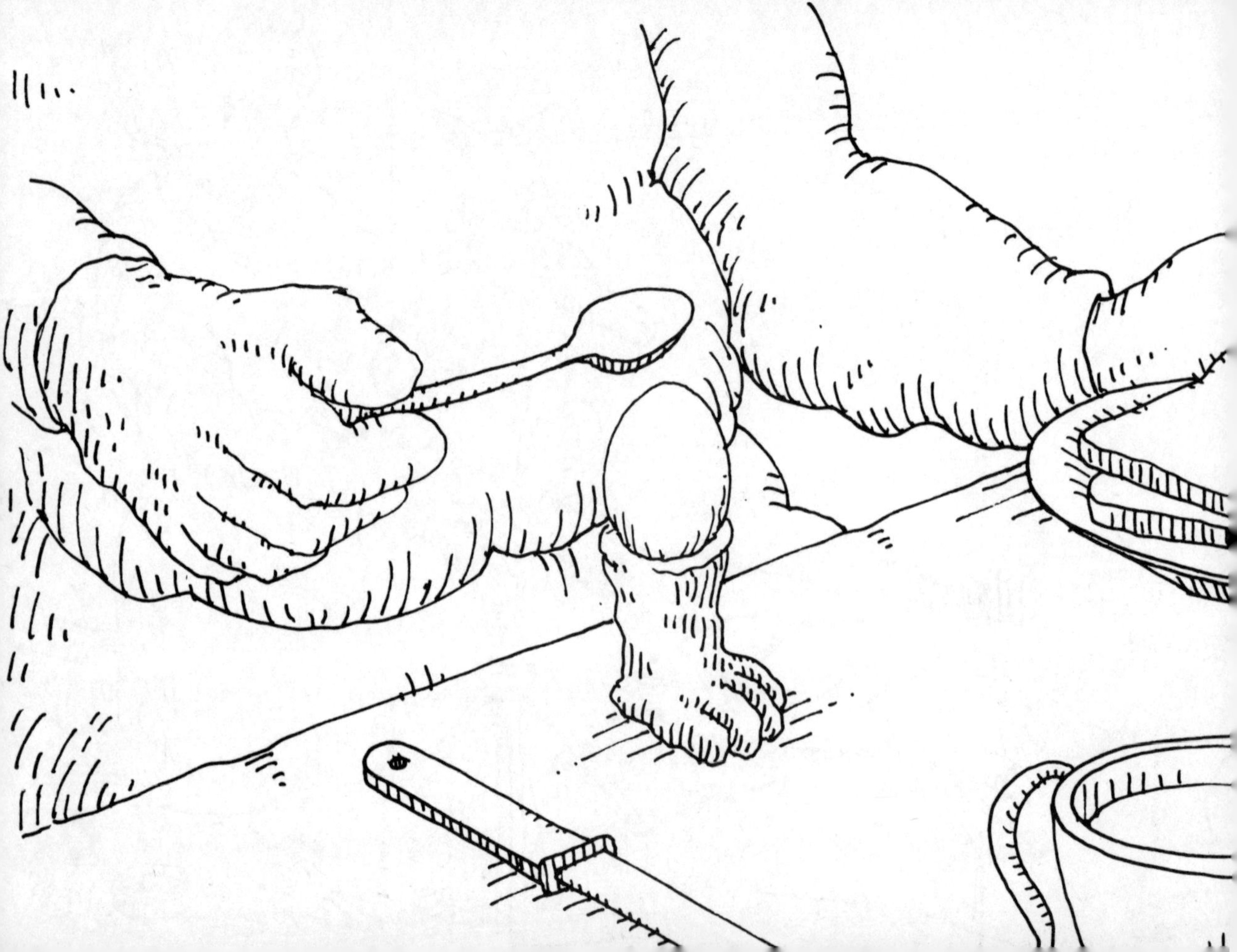

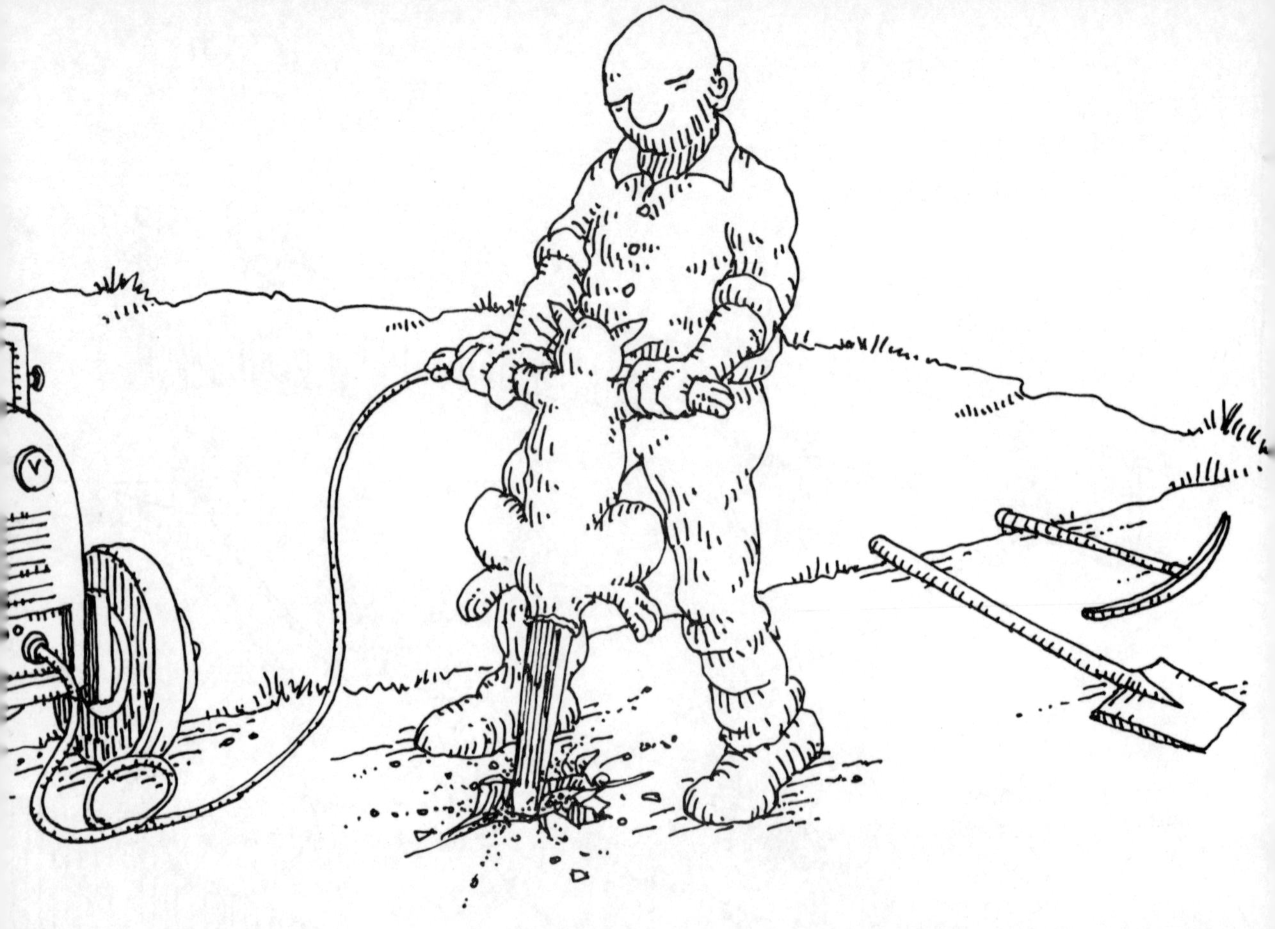

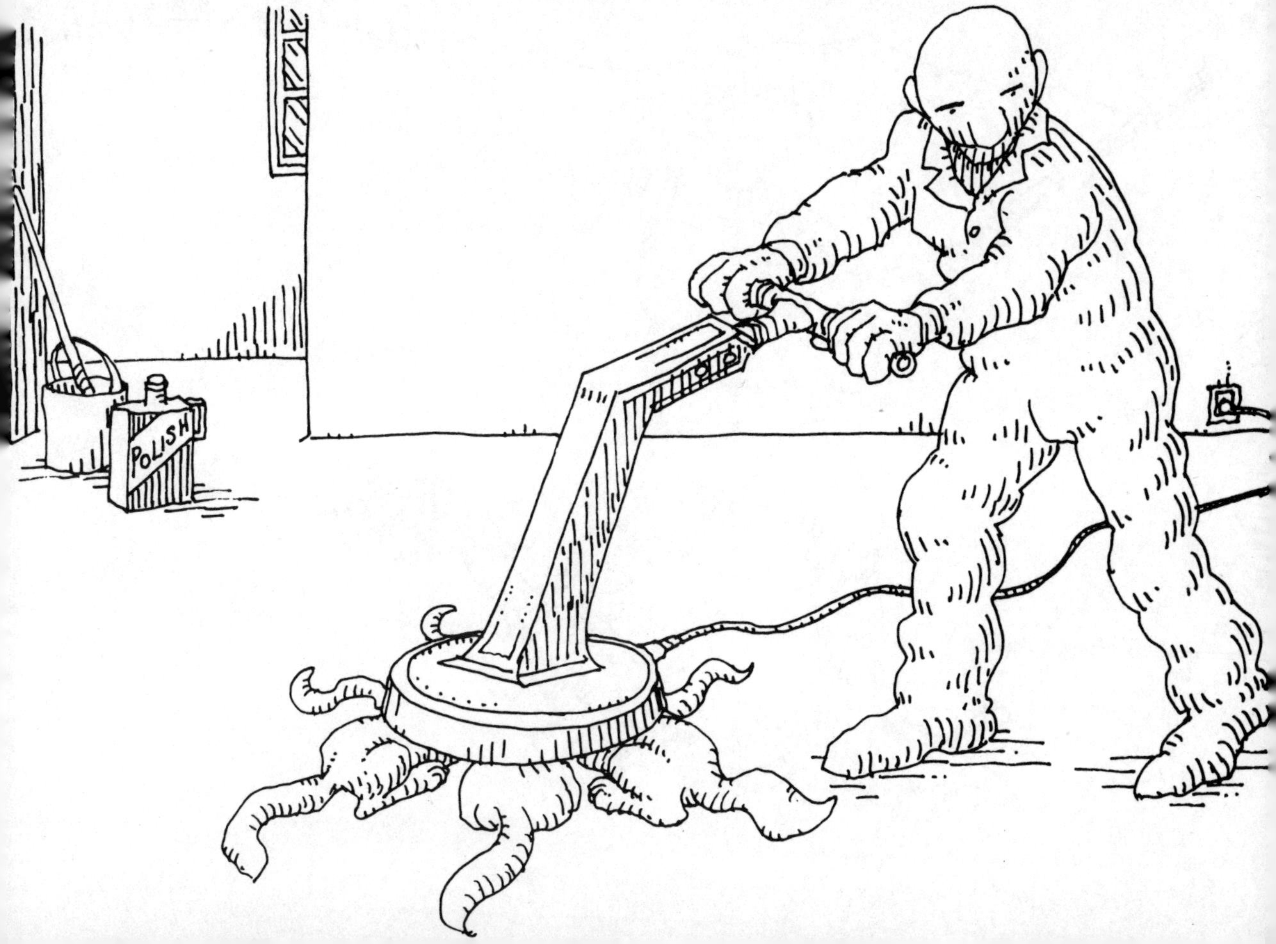
POLISH

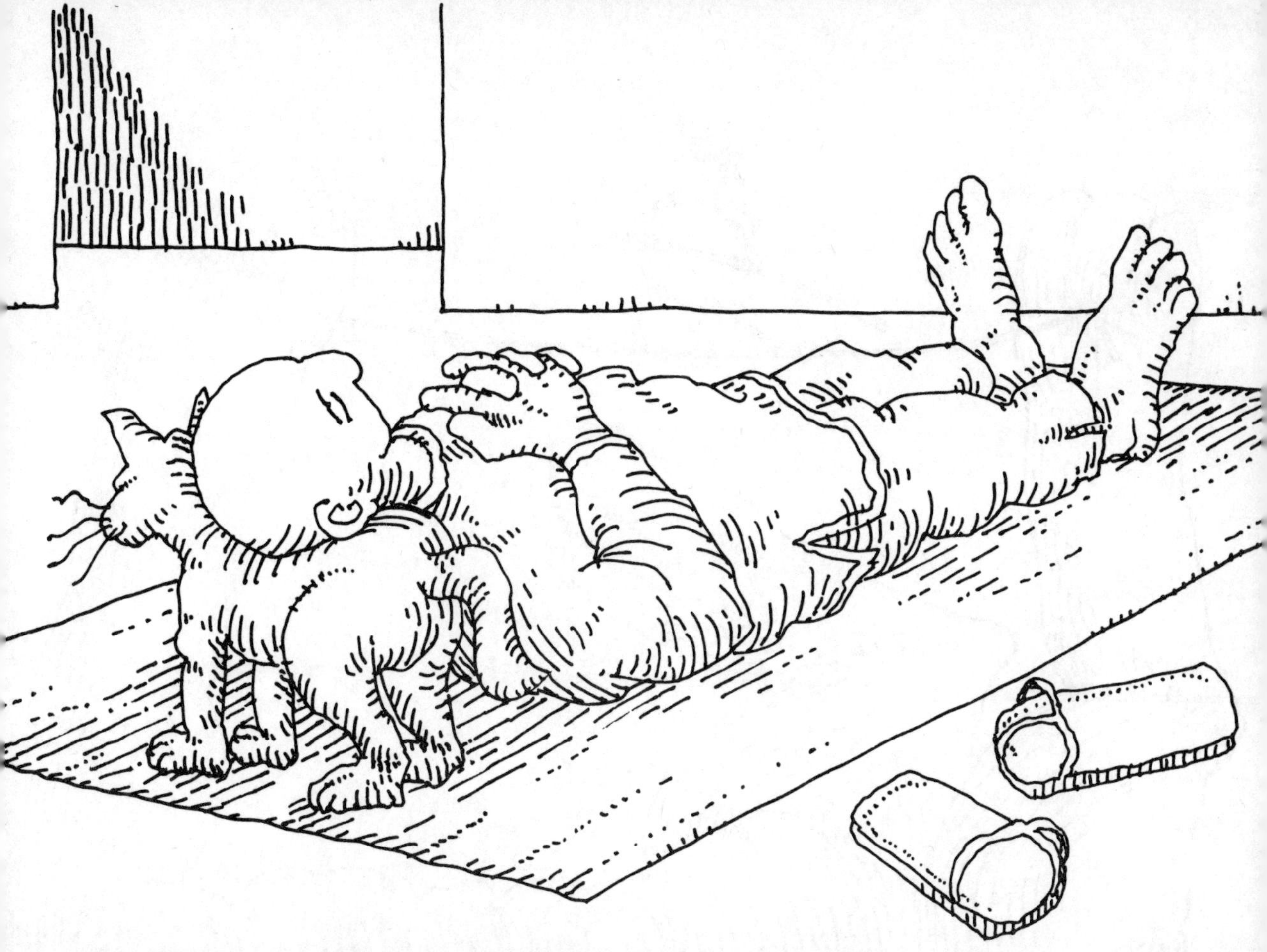

SUN
SUN
CLOUDY
RAI
CLOUDY
TOMORROW

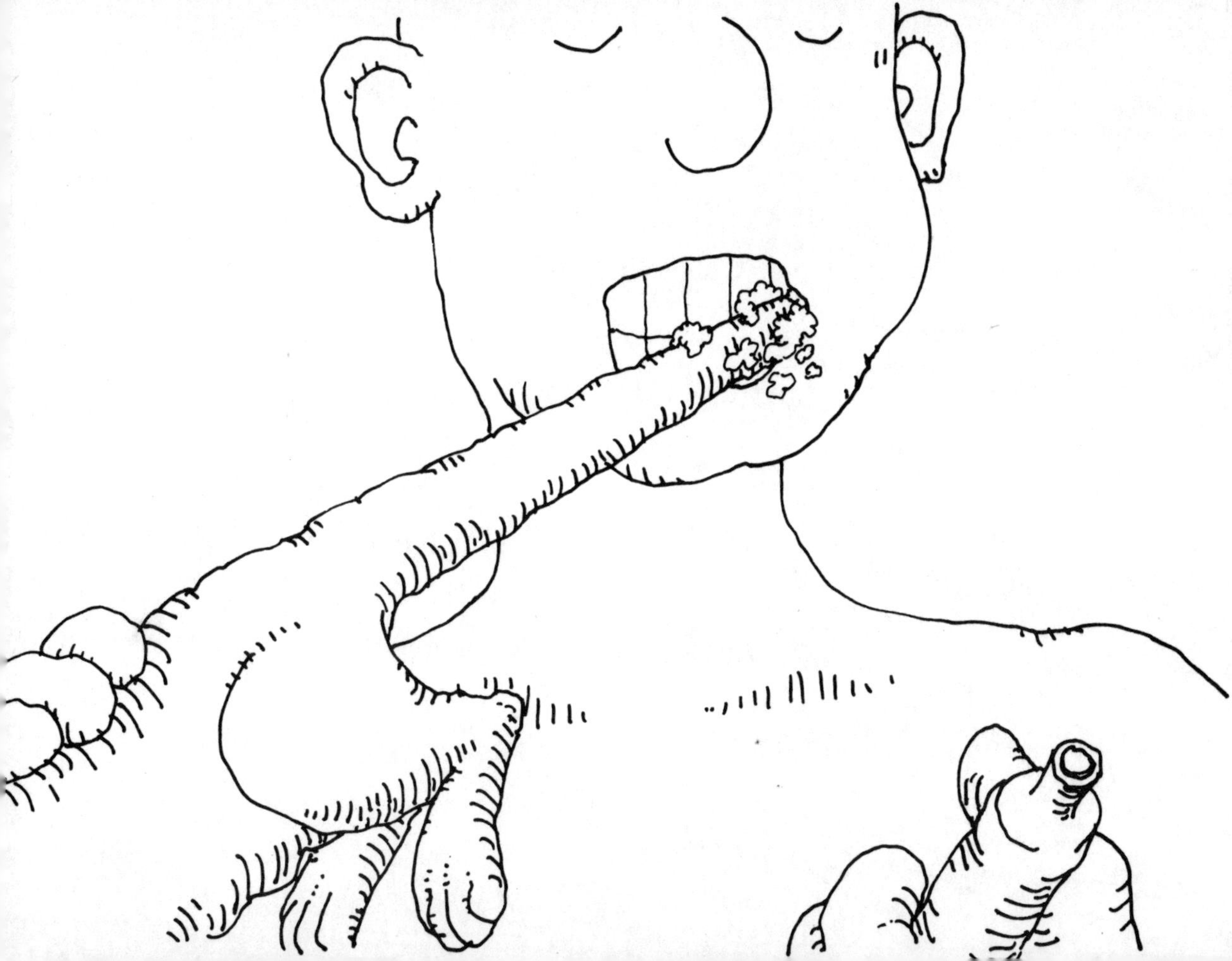

21

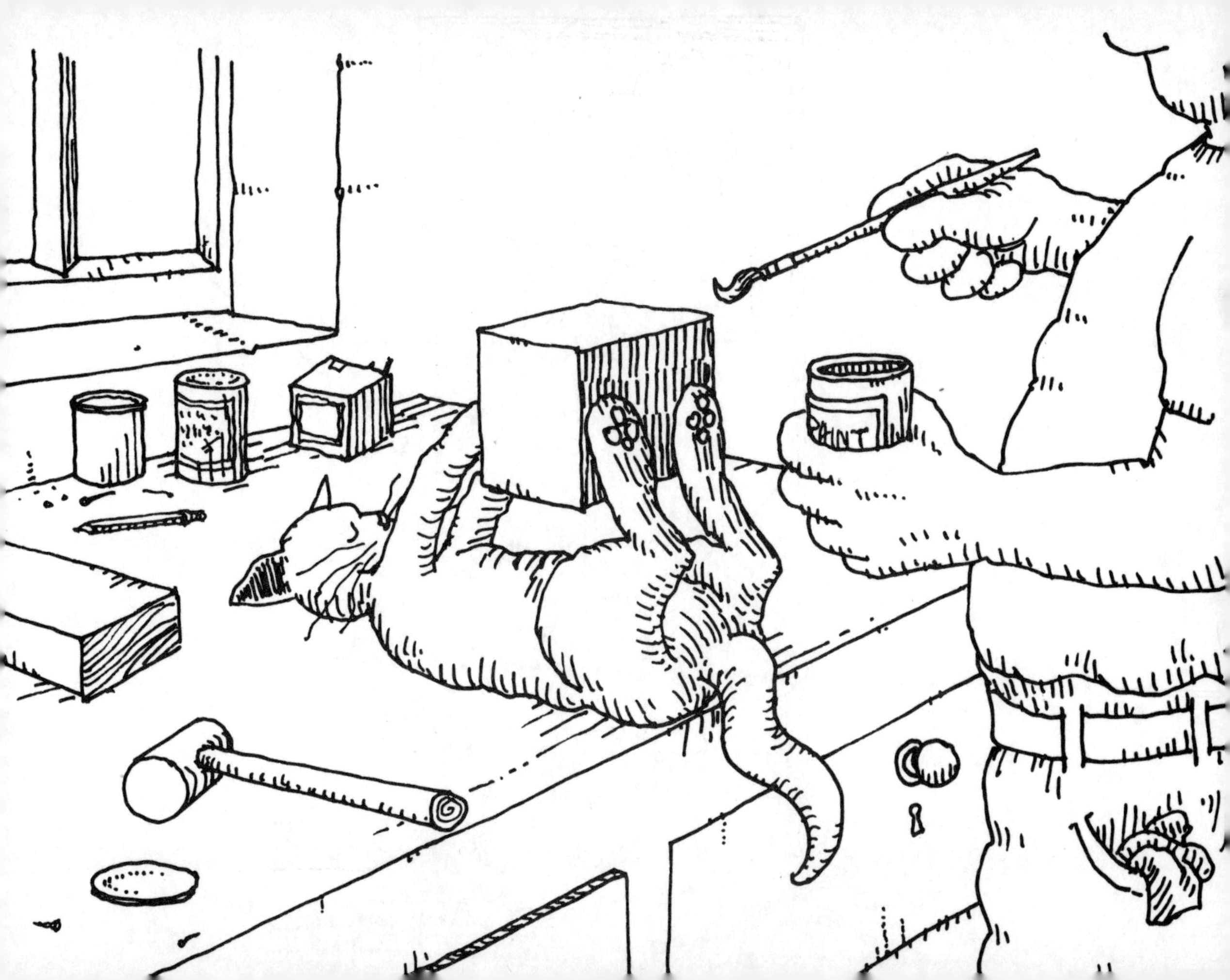
PAINT

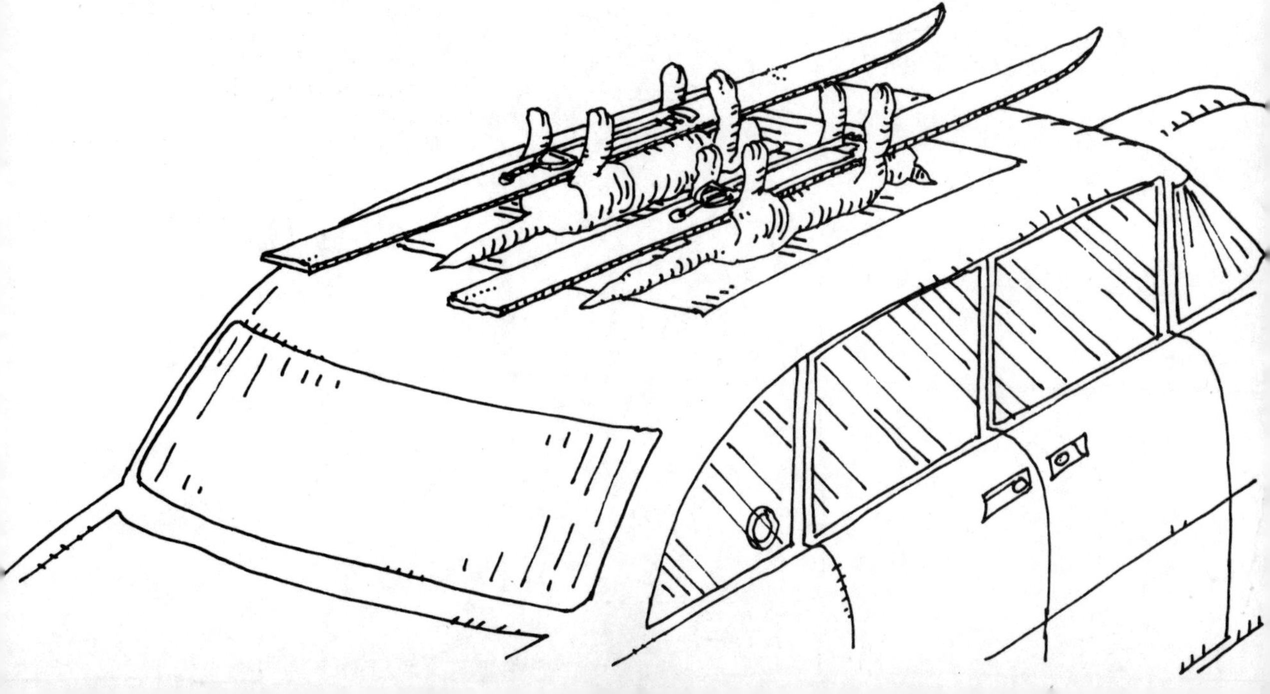

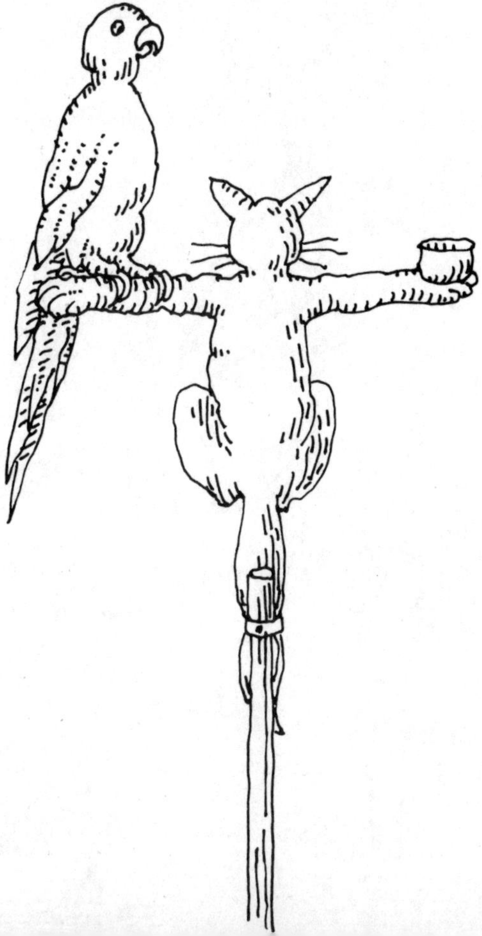

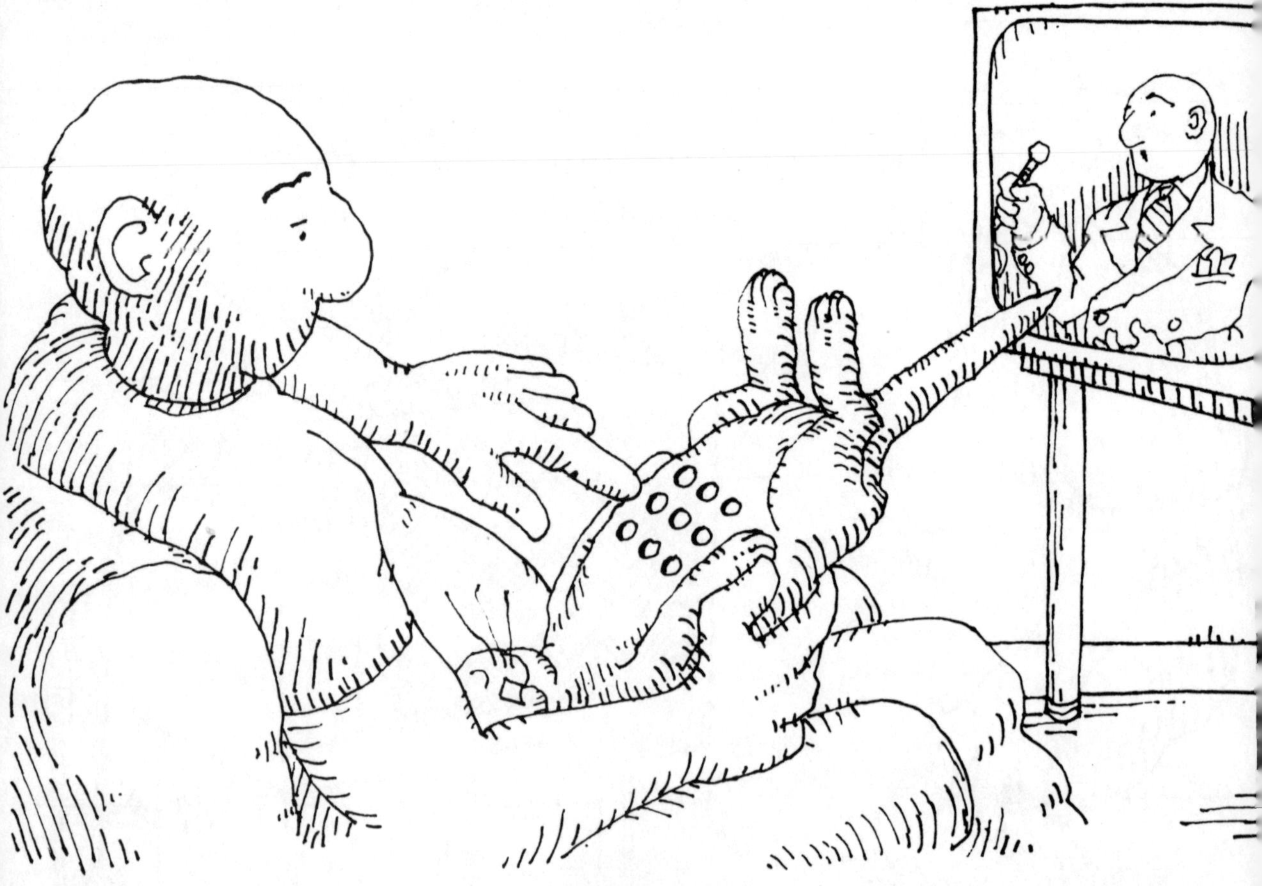

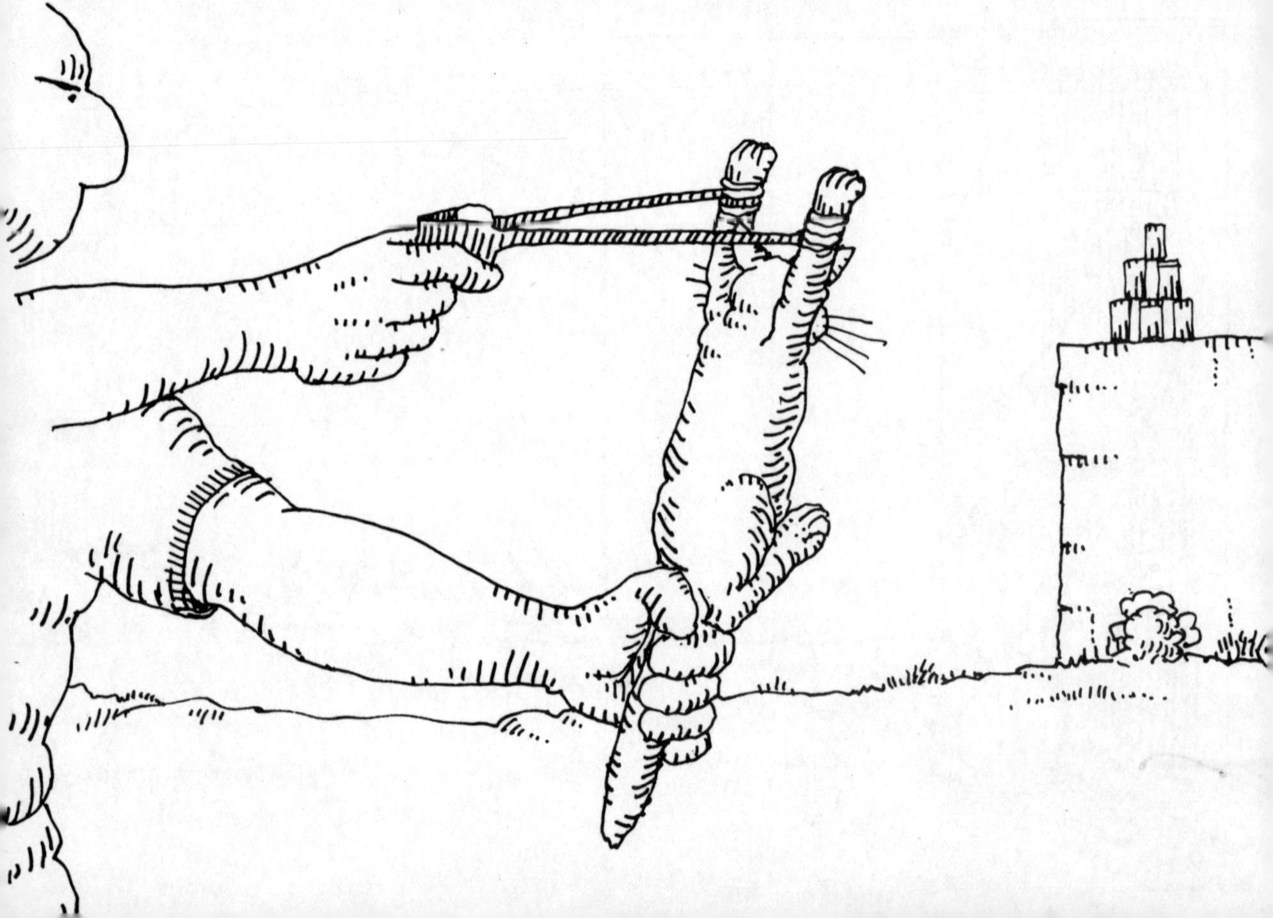

734

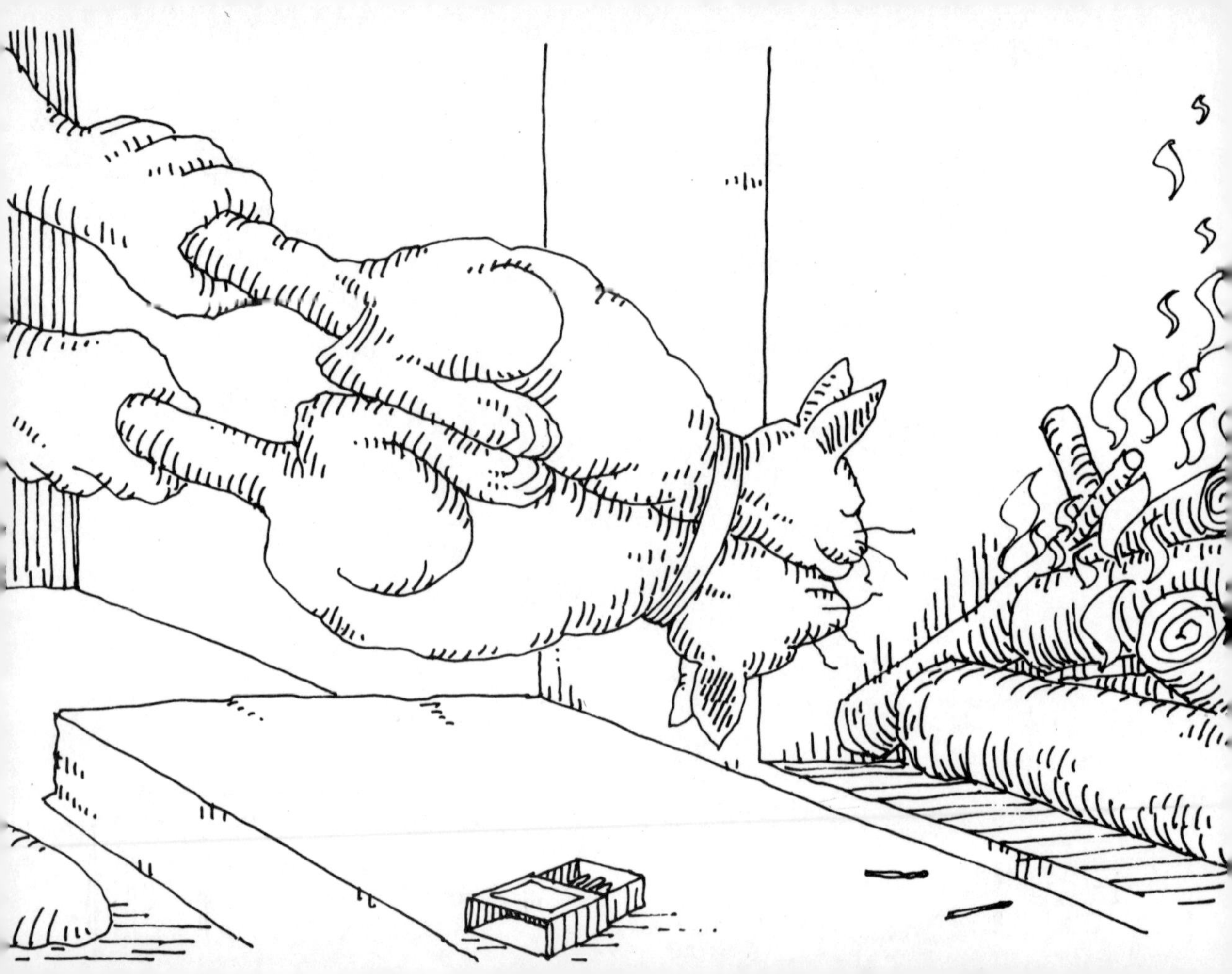

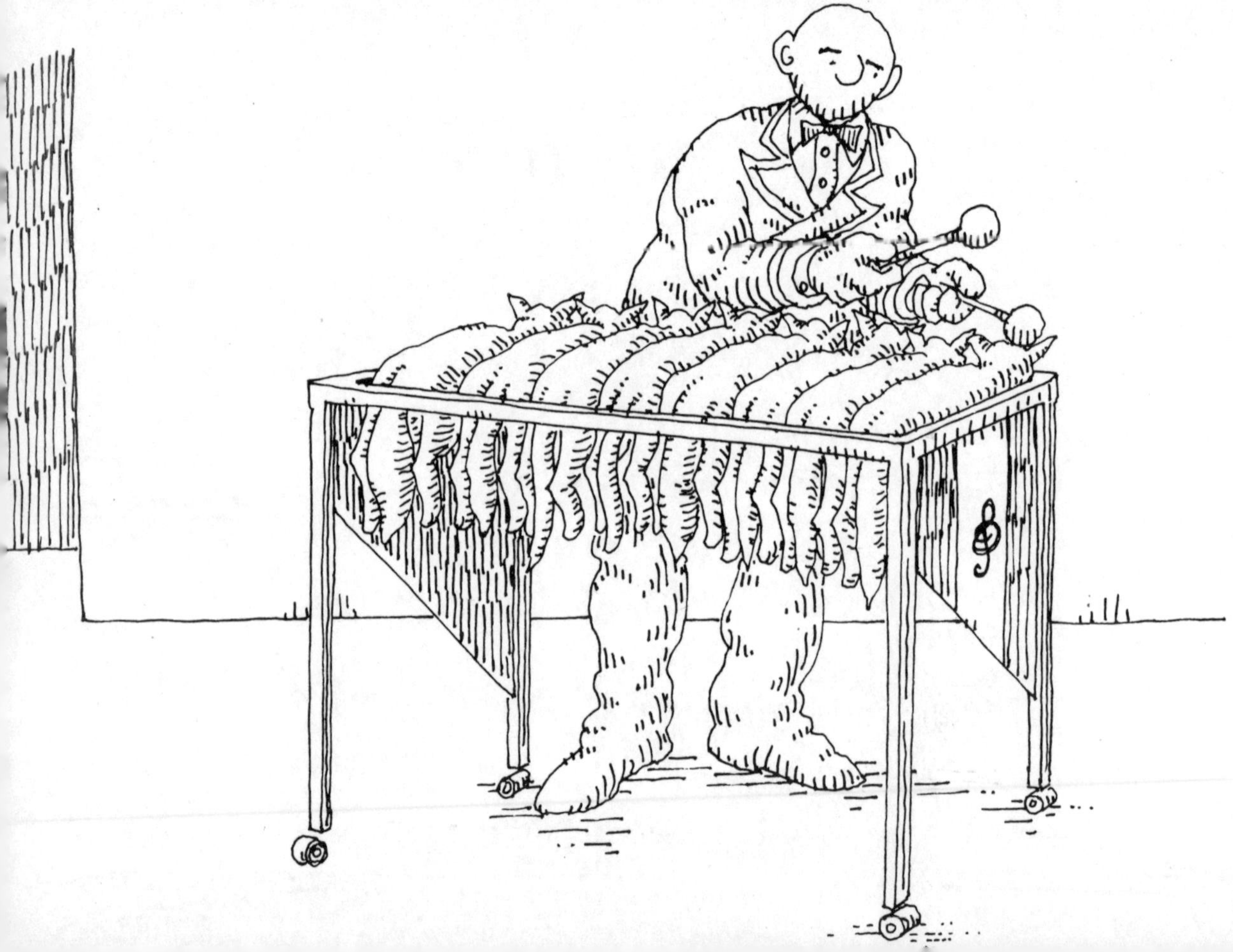